IMAGES
of America

JOHN O'HARA'S
ANTHRACITE
REGION

John Henry O'Hara (1905–1970), the American author from Pottsville, Schuylkill County, Pennsylvania, put his ethnographical, geographical, and historical knowledge about "The Region" into a novelistic form. Besides being a literary artist, O'Hara, truly, deserves the titles of ethnographer, geographer, and social historian within his biographical sketch. His epitaph summed him up best of all:

> Better than anyone else, he told the truth about his time, the first half of the twentieth century. He was a professional. He wrote honestly and well.
>
> (Bruccoli, *The O'Hara Concern* 339)

IMAGES
of America

John O'Hara's Anthracite Region

Pamela C. Mac Arthur, D.Phil.

ARCADIA
PUBLISHING

Copyright © 1999 by Pamela C. Mac Arthur, D.Phil
ISBN 978-1-5316-0227-7

Published by Arcadia Publishing
Charleston, South Carolina

Library of Congress Catalog Card Number: Applied for.

For all general information contact Arcadia Publishing at:
Telephone 843-853-2070
Fax 843-853-0044
E-Mail sales@arcadiapublishing.com
For customer service and orders:
Toll-Free 1-888-313-2665

Visit us on the Internet at www.arcadiapublishing.com

To the left of the photograph is seen the young serious-looking 20-year-old cub reporter, John O'Hara. In 1925, who would have realized John O'Hara's destiny? At that time, he was the cub reporter who would rather take a girl out on the town than write up a piece on a church supper (or such topic) in Schuylkill County.

Contents

Acknowledgments 6

Introduction 7

1. "The Anthracite Region" through John O'Hara's Eyes 9

2. O'Hara's "Gibbsville," Pottsville, Pennsylvania 25

3. The "Aristocrats'" Way of Life in Lantenengo County (Schuylkill County) 53

4. The "Aristocrats'" Schooling Inside and Outside "The Region" 67

5. The "Aristocrats'" Social Enclaves and Escapes 87

Acknowledgments

I would like to thank "The Region's" inhabitants for assuring me that a glance at O'Hara's work would gladly give rise to the "Truth " of "The Region." From patrons of coffee shops to grocery stores, I have had moral support to continue on with my Life's work on John Henry O'Hara, the so-called wastrel from Pottsville, Schuylkill County, Pennsylvania.

My family—my twin sister Nancy E. Karvellas, my "baby" sister Heidi F. Schubert, and sister Karen Grizzard—have on countless occasions supported me when there was no support, but an apathy towards my "on-going concern" of O'Hara; my grandmother's (Violette T. Beale-Edgley) and mother's principles bolstered me. Countless acquaintances have reassured me that this encounter with O'Hara again is not in vain. I wish to wholeheartedly thank my Pottsvillian friend, Mrs. Terri LaPlaca, who gave me continual support throughout the "last" years of my Doctoral Programme and my concerns about O'Hara. My dear friend, Mrs. "B" (Bernadette Koury Barket, a Pottsvillian through and through), who supplied me with her knowledge about "The Region"; her own personal collection of "The Region's" history; countless hours of her time during this effort and who also gave me the inspiration "to carry on" when time became of the essence, I gratefully thank. I would like to especially thank my friend, Charles Strange, the author of *Mountain Majesties*, who has continually supported me in my efforts on John O'Hara. I thank my friend, Jack Knarr, who has given me a continual boost throughout the years that I have worked on O'Hara. I wish to thank the Historical Society of Schuylkill County for giving me the permission to utilize the photographs of John Henry O'Hara. I also give thanks to my friend, Lois A. Tamke, who gave me the moral support throughout my concern with Pottsville's John Henry O'Hara, and to whom I dedicate *John O'Hara's Anthracite Region*. Last but not least, I thank my editor, Heather Gunsalus, for sustaining me throughout this task, and editor Peter Turko, for his moral support during the final days of completing this work.

INTRODUCTION

John O'Hara's Anthracite Region covers the exciting period from the 1880s to 1945 in the coal region of Pennsylvania. Through John Henry O'Hara's eyes, the ethnography, geography, and social history of "The Anthracite Region" (so-called "The Region" by its inhabitants), particularly the American author's hometown, Pottsville (Gibbsville), and his home county of Schuylkill County (Lantenengo County in his Pennsylvania novels, novellas, and short stories) is portrayed. A personal collection of photographs and early century postcards illustrates O'Hara's "aristocratic" view of his "Pennsylvania Protectorate." Through his upper-class characters such as Joseph B. Chapin and Martha Sterling Downs, O'Hara has given an accurate portrayal of the lives of the wealthy in Pennsylvania in the first half of the American Twentieth Century. From the "Aristocrats' " escape to Eagles Mere, Sullivan County, to the amusement parks such as Tumbling Run and Marlin Park in "The Anthracite Region," O'Hara captured the upper class's way of life. The social enclaves such as The Out Door Club, The Pottsville Club, and The Schuylkill Country Club, and the fashionable attire, automobiles, houses, and schools of the day are given due attention. One can truly see a remarkable re-creation of "The Region" in the O'Hara Canon.

Matthew J. Bruccoli claimed that O'Hara "was one of our best novelists, our best novellaist, and our greatest writer of short stories."[1] If one puts the literary artist aside, and examines O'Hara's body of work from another perspective, John Henry O'Hara defined "The Region" and its people within it so satisfactorily that the ethnographers, geographers, and historians must take a look at his work. For, not to do so would omit an essential part of the American cultural and historical heritage. O'Hara's view of "The Region" may not meet everyone's approval, but it is a vision—a vision of a man who sought the truth. For this, no one can scorn him. And if one can bear the use of obscenities and, at times, long-winded passages within his literature, and burrow beneath this surface, one can truly see a record of the upper to lower classes in Pennsylvania between 1880 and 1945 and a re-creation of "The Region."[2] In John Henry O'Hara's own words, his purpose in the writing of his fiction was summed up as follows:

> . . . In middle age I was proud to have lived according to my emotions at the right time, and content to live that way vicariously and at a distance. I had missed almost nothing, escaped very little, and at fifty I had begun to devote my energy and time to the last, simple but big task of putting it all down as well as I knew how.[3]

John Henry O'Hara underestimated himself. He recorded "The Anthracite Region's" ethnography, geography, and history from his very first novel onwards. (*Appointment in Samarra* 16 August 1934) The American author from Pottsville, Schuylkill County, Pennsylvania, put his homestate and particularly "The Anthracite Region" (specifically within a 30-mile radius of Pottsville) under a microscope and accurately reported its upper class's most intimate aspects from 1880 to 1945 in his Pennsylvania novels: *Appointment in Samarra*, *Ten North Frederick*, *Ourselves to Know*, and *The Lockwood Concern*. On occasion, "The Anthracite Region" appeared in *A Rage to Live*, *From the Terrace*, and *Pal Joey*.

This photographic layout of O'Hara's work (his Pennsylvania novels, novellas, and short stories) is done in hope that one of America's most neglected authors may be re-examined from a pleasurable standpoint, and, possibly, an academic one as well. If one person steps into O'Hara's World, this cursory glance at it has not been in vain.

End Notes

1. Matthew J. Bruccoli, *The O'Hara Concern: A Biography of John O'Hara* (1975; Pittsburgh: University of Pittsburgh Press, 1995) 345.

2. Pamela C. Mac Arthur, "John Henry O'Hara's View of the Upper Classes in Pennsylvania Between 1900 and 1930" (Dissertation, University of Alberta, 1986) 110; Pamela C. Mac Arthur, "John O'Hara: A Biographical Study" (Dissertation, University of Sussex, Brighton, England, 1999) 179; Thomas Patrick Coakley, " 'O'Hara Country' Revisited: A Study of Regionalism, Theme and Point of View in the Work of John O'Hara" (Dissertation, Pennsylvania State University, 1983) 23-24; Matthew J. Bruccoli, ed., *Gibbsville,PA*, with a preface by George V. Higgins and an introduction by Matthew J. Bruccoli (New York: Carroll & Graf, 1992) 17.

3. John O'Hara, "Imagine Kissing Pete," *Sermons and Soda-Water*, with a foreword by John O'Hara (1960; New York: Carroll & Graf, 1986) 72.

One

"THE ANTHRACITE REGION" THROUGH JOHN O'HARA'S EYES

John Henry O'Hara, the American author from Pottsville, Schuylkill County, Pennsylvania, re-created "The Anthracite Region" in his Pennsylvania novels, novellas, and short stories. O'Hara's world was so engrained in him that he not only referred to this area that stretched from Scranton to Pottsville (Gibbsville) in his body of work, but in his personal correspondence as well. He, specifically, zoned in on the cities, towns, villages, and patches that were within a 30-mile radius from his beloved hometown, Pottsville, located in Schuylkill County (Lantenengo County). O'Hara diligently reported in his first novel:

> ... The anthracite region lies roughly between Scranton on the north and Gibbsville on the south. In fact Point Mountain [Sharp Mountain], upon which Gibbsville's earliest settlement was made, is the delight of geologists, who come from as far away as Germany to examine Gibbsville Conglomerate [Pottsville Conglomerate], a stone formation found nowhere else in the world. When that geological squeeze, or whatever it was that produced veins of coal, occurred, it did not go south of Point Mountain, and coal is found on the north slope of Point Mountain, but not on the south side, and at the eastern face of Point Mountain is found Gibbsville Conglomerate. The richest veins of anthracite in the world are within a thirty-mile sector from Gibbsville, and when those veins are being worked, Gibbsville prospers. When the mines are idle, Gibbsville puts on a long face and begins to think in terms of soup kitchens. (*Appointment in Samarra* 49)

This is a splendid view of Sharp Mountain (looking east) which contained the Pottsville Conglomerate ("Gibbsville Conglomerate") on its eastern face and anthracite coal on its northern slope. (*Appointment in Samarra* 49)

> . . . The gang would go out on the mountain and play "Tarzan of the Apes," jumping around from tree to tree and skinning their behinds on the bark. You had to be careful on the mountains, careful of airholes, which were treacherous, or supposed to be treacherous, places where the ground was undermined and liable to cave in. In the memory of the oldest citizen of Gibbsville no life had been lost in Gibbsville as a result of a mine cave-in, but the danger was there. (*Appointment in Samarra* 150)

Pottsville, O'Hara's "Gibbsville," viewed from the top of Sharp Mountain (Point Mountain) was a magnificent sight at the beginning of the century. John O'Hara's world with its Schuylkill County Courthouse, church spires, and surrounding hills captivated the young boy's imagination; consequently, O'Hara wrote about his hometown for the rest of his life.

From the eastern face of Sharp Mountain (Point Mountain) in Pottsville (Gibbsville), one can see how the Schuylkill Valley looked with its dirt roads, Schuylkill River, Schuylkill Canal, and boxcars in the early days of the century.

> . . . Sometimes the gang would sit on the rocks on the mountain and watch the coal trains coming down the valley from the east, and they would count the cars: seventy-eight battleship cars was the highest number they ever saw and agreed upon . . . (*Appointment in Samarra* 150).

When John O'Hara was born at 125 Mahantongo Street in 1905, the Schuylkill Valley looking east from the top of Sharp Mountain (Point Mountain) appeared to be a "tranquil" spot surrounded by mountains.

A train going south on the track through the Schuylkill Valley to Schuylkill Haven left a lot to be desired for Julian English and the gang.

> ... It was a cold and dangerous ride, and about once a year some boy would fall off and lose a leg or be killed under the wheels, but the practice of hopping coalies went on. It was not wise to go beyond Swedish Haven [Schuylkill Haven], because after that the railroad veered off too far from the highway ... (*Appointment in Samarra* 151).

A train makes its way near Cape Horn, Pottsville, in the Schuylkill Valley.
   . . . Sometimes they [gang] would go down in the valley and when the train slowed up or stopped at Gibbsville Junction [Pottsville] they would get on and ride . . . the five miles to Swedish Haven [Schuylkill Haven] . . . There was a coalie that slowed down at Gibbsville Junction every day at about three-fifteen, and it reached Swedish Haven at four o'clock, . . . (*Appointment in Samarra* 151).

No doubt, Julian English and his gang saw this track of the Pennsylvania Railroad when they were on their various journeys in the Valley. (*Appointment in Samarra* 150-151)

These railroad yards at Cressona were seen by Julian English and the gang on their way to Schuylkill Haven when they decided to hop the coalies. (*Appointment in Samarra* 150-151)

West West Falls, Minersville (Collieryville) was a "spot" that young lovers such as Isabel Barley and Jim, her "sporadic lover," formerly from Gibbsville, perhaps, visited to have their romantic interludes. ("A Few Trips and Some Poetry" 105)

In 1908, the people of Port Carbon used the Coal Street Bridge to cross over the waters of the Schuylkill. Possibly, the town of Port Carbon is O'Hara's steel town of Port Johnson in *From the Terrace* even though O'Hara claimed Pottstown was it. After all, a steel foundry was located on Mill and Main Streets at the beginning of the century. (*Selected Letters of JOHN O'HARA*, John O'Hara to Charles Poore, 7 June 1958, 273; Elmer Drumheller, telephone interview, Pottsville, Pennsylvania to Port Carbon, Pennsylvania, 19 July 1999)

During the winter of 1922–23, 18-year-old John O'Hara frequently travelled the Main Street of St. Clair on the way to Frackville to see his sweetheart, Gladys Suender. (John O'Hara, letter to Miss Mary Connelly, 16 June 1962; John O'Hara Papers, The Rare Books Room, Pattee Library, Pennsylvania State University, State College, Pennsylvania)

Frackville was O'Hara's Mountain City of *From the Terrace* and his short story "Zero." Alfred Eaton of *From the Terrace* would meet Natalie Benziger, the daughter of the general superintendent of the Mountain City Coal Company, in surroundings such as this. (*From the Terrace* 491) Even the young John O'Hara zoomed up to Frackville in one of Dr. Patrick O'Hara's automobiles to meet with Gladys Suender and Jean Taggert. (John O'Hara, letter to Miss Mary Connelly, 16 June 1962; John O'Hara Papers, The Rare Books Room, Pattee Library, Pennsylvania State University, State College, Pennsylvania) (*Selected Letters of JOHN O'HARA*, John O'Hara to Robert Simonds, 1923, 11)

When Alfred Eaton came to see Natalie Benziger in Mountain City (Frackville), he would have seen houses similar to the homes on Nice Street. When visiting his Frackville friends in the winter of 1922–1923, John O'Hara would have, probably, travelled down this picturesque street. (John O'Hara, letter to Miss Mary Connelly, 16 June 1962; John O'Hara Papers, The Rare Books Room, Pattee Library, Pennsylvania State University, State College, Pennsylvania) (*Selected Letters of JOHN O'HARA*, John O'Hara to Robert Simonds, 1923, 11)

In 1920, Center Street in Mahanoy City was bustling. The trolley car transported the average citizen down its main thoroughfare to shop in its 5 and 10¢ store to the left of the scene. One group of O'Hara's favorite musicians—The Dorsey Brothers—played in this area of the coal region. No doubt, O'Hara thought about this when he wrote *From the Terrace* in 1958.

This South White Street scene of 1930 illustrates the type of environment that John O'Hara's father's family lived in at the beginning of the twentieth century. The O'Hara family lived at Lloyd and White Streets during Shenandoah's boom times.

When John O'Hara and his friends went up to Hazleton to eat, drink, and dance, they drove streets such as this in their fathers' automobiles. It was likely that O'Hara drove down this street. He always loved to venture out to a hot spot such as Papa Turin's in West Hazleton and then carouse about afterwards. (*Selected Letters of JOHN O'HARA*, John O'Hara to Robert Simonds, December 1932, 72-73)

The "Coal Barons" of Pottsville delighted in their business excursions up to Scranton in the earlier part of the century. "Coal Business" meant Money, and why not visit a pleasant city such as this? The "Anthracite" and old-monied men of Scranton-Wilkes Barre met with various types of gentlemen at the private clubs in Harrisburg (Fort Penn) and attended funerals such as Joseph B. Chapin's in Gibbsville (Pottsville). (*A Rage to Live* 58-59) (*Ten North Frederick* 23-24)

In 1907, Scranton which was the tip of "The Anthracite Region," had its imposing mansions. This particular home located on Vine Street was owned by Colonel E.H. Ripple.

In *Appointment in Samarra*, O'Hara spoke about the vein of anthracite that stretched from Scranton to the north side of Sharp Mountain (Point Mountain) in Pottsville. The Bellevue Coal Breaker in Scranton was typical of its time (1911) and, certainly, was one of many in "The Region." (*Appointment in Samarra* 49)

The Schuylkill County Fair Grounds in Cressona was a place that the 18-year-old John O'Hara visited. The Fair was such a significant event in 1923 when it first appeared that O'Hara called the town of Cressona "Fair Grounds" in his semi-autobiographical short story "Imagine Kissing Pete." Note the beauty of the scenery in Cressona. (Pottsville Sesquicentennial 1806–1956, 77)

This view of Schuylkill Haven (Swedish Haven) was the Schuykill Haven of O'Hara's childhood and George Lockwood's young manhood in 1911.

> . . . Swedish Haven [Schuylkill Haven], although it was only a few miles from Gibbsville, was not considered to belong to the coal region. It was the last Pennsylvania Dutch town on the way northward, and Gibbsville was the first coal town . . . (*The Lockwood Concern* 229; Coakley, " 'O'Hara Country' Revisited": See Bibliography 18).

Edith Chapin and her children would visit Main Street, Schuylkill Haven (Swedish Haven) for ice cream at Franz's Confectionery and Ice Cream Parlor (Michael's Confectionery and Ice Cream Parlor) when staying out at the farm outside of Orwigsburg in the hot, summer months. (*Ten North Frederick* 253) (Jane Sharadin, telephone interview, Pottsville, Pennsylvania, 19 July 1999)

> ... A trip to Swedish Haven in the ice-wagon became an adventure, climaxed with an ice cream soda at Franz's ... (*Ten North Frederick* 243).

St. Matthew's Church on Dock Street, Schuylkill Haven (Swedish Haven), was only a few squares away from Moses Lockwood's office on Dock Street.

> ... He [Moses Lockwood] had become so enfeebled that he seldom made the effort to walk the few squares to his office in Dock Street, and business matters that required his attention were taken care of at his desk in the den in the red brick box ... (*The Lockwood Concern* 114).

In 1893, Dr. Patrick O'Hara "was elected by the Directors of the Poor of Schuylkill County to take charge of the hospital [Schuylkill County Hospital for Insane] in connection with the county alms-house [Schuylkill County Almshouse] and [to become] superintendent of the insane asylum; . . ." (Samuel T. Wiley, *Biographical And Portrait Cyclopedia Of Schuylkill County Pennsylvania* 243)

John O'Hara wrote about the insane asylum in *The Lockwood Concern*:

> . . . There had been no way to avoid telling the Hoffner family that Daphne Lockwood was in the crazy-house, the *Insane*, as it was also called; but Rhoda's advanced condition had been a secret . . . (*The Lockwood Concern* 106).

This Schuylkill County Almshouse near Schuylkill Haven was a "haven" for the poor of Schuylkill County. Its pleasant surroundings with its cows in the meadow soothed its charges.

During O'Hara's months (January to March 1927) at the *Tamaqua Courier*, he would, occasionally, have a $1.25 dinner at the Majestic Hotel on East Broad Street, Tamaqua (Taqua). Surely, O'Hara took part in the dining and dancing activities in Tamaqua during the winter months of 1927. (Advertising in the *Tamaqua Courier*, 1 February to 21 March, 1927)

The Market Street Bridge in Lykens (Lyons) had its daily foot traffic along with its vehicular transportation crossing over it in the early part of the century. O'Hara's characters, Robert Millhouser and Hedda Steele, in *Ourselves to Know*, used this bridge in their daily walks. (*Ourselves to Know* 234)

Two

O'Hara's "Gibbsville,"
Pottsville, Pennsylvania

John O'Hara's "Gibbsville," Pottsville "was reachable by highway, railway, and the canal, but these transportation lines had been cut through a dense forest; snake, panther, and wildcat country, and on occasion bear . . ." (*The Lockwood Concern* 80). Historically, O'Hara recorded that Gibbsville "was refounded in 1806" and gradually evolved into a "third class city" in 1911. (*Appointment in Samarra* 52; 207) By 1945, O'Hara categorized Gibbsville as a "bastard town":

> . . . so many of the so-called first families, they don't seem to have anything to do with coal. Some of them own farms, some own timber land. Small factories. The steel mill. Silk mill. Shirt factories. It's a highly skilled town . . . (*Ten North Frederick* 57-58).

John O'Hara was so caught up with his hometown of Pottsville that he examined it as if he put it under a microscope. With his penchant for accuracy, he not only recorded its history, but its geographical layout and ethnography. Whether he was documenting the "Aristocrats" who lived on North Frederick Street (North George Street), South Centre Street (South Main Street), Mahantongo Street (Lantenengo Street), or Oak Road (Twin Oaks Road) or the middle classes on Norwegian Street (Christiana Street) and Market Street (West Market Street) or the lower classes on the east side of the railroad tracks near the ugly railroad district, O'Hara knew exactly where his Gibbsvillians lived, their family's history, and the class of society into which they were born. He was so smitten with "Gibbsville" that he permanently left its mark in literature.[1]

1. Thomas Patrick Coakley, " 'O'Hara Country' Revisited: A Study of Regionalism, Theme and Point of View in the Work of John O'Hara" (Dissertation, Pennsylvania State University, 1983) 23-24.

These views of Pottsville encompass John O'Hara's childhood world from St. Patrick's Church at 319 Mahantongo Street to his father's, Dr. Patrick O'Hara, workplace—The Pottsville Hospital. O'Hara was so inspired by his majestic-looking hometown surrounded by seven "mountains" that he wrote about Pottsville's ethnography, history, and topography in his Pennsylvania novels, novellas, and short stories throughout his life.

In this view facing south from the Schuylkill County Courthouse, one can see the eastern face of Sharp Mountain, which contained the "Pottsville Conglomerate" ("Gibbsville Conglomerate") and its northern slope, which held the deposits of anthracite. In 1909, the Borough of Pottsville appeared to be congested with houses and buildings beneath the northern slope of Sharp Mountain (Point Mountain) in this scene. (*Appointment in Samarra* 49)

During Edith Chapin's day (1911), this north-east view of Pottsville shows that the houses and buildings were surrounded by the industries of the day—railroad, steel, and timber—and the majestic mountains.

The "East Side" of Pottsville housed the "Aristocrats" such as Joseph B. Chapin at 10 North Frederick Street (North George Street). At the upper right of the view, one can see a sign that is advertising the lots for sale on the top of Greenwood Hill in East Pottsville.

This bird's-eye view of Pottsville from Race Street School illustrates the types of housing in Pottsville in 1905 when John O'Hara was born.

In this view of Jalappa, Pottsville, in 1916, one can see houses and industries mixed together. The meat-packing house of Jacob Ulmer was located on Water and Front Streets across from some of his workers' houses. O'Hara was quite aware that the owners of the meat-packing plants in Pottsville lived in American luxury and, definitely, not like their workers. (*Ten North Frederick* 119)

One can see the majestic Academy of Music located on the lower end of Mahantongo Street (Lantenengo). The O'Haras attended the various musical functions that occurred in this institution up until 1914. (It burnt down on 17 December 1914.) From these early encounters

John O'Hara would have taken the Cressona Road on the south end of Pottsville when riding his five-gaited mare "Julia" out to Dr. Patrick O'Hara's Panther Valley farm. In "A Few Trips and Some Poetry," he related that "[he] would stop at the trough in front of the Farmers Hotel [Beckville] and let [his] mare have a few sips of water . . ." after his journey along the Cressona Road. ("A Few Trips and Some Poetry" 38)

with music, John O'Hara developed a lifelong appreciation of it. (Pottsville Sesquicentennial 1806–1956, 54)

On the left side of Centre Street (Main), one can see the Hotel Allan, forerunner of the Necho Allen, which opened on 1 November 1927 (John Gibb Hotel, "Gibbsville's big inn"), on the southwestern corner of Mahantongo (Lantenengo) and Centre (Main) Streets. This hotel was managed by Clyde Allan. (*Pottsville Sesquicentennial 1806–1956*, 39) (*Appointment in Samarra* 33)

The Hotel Allan (on the left) was a welcoming sight for the upper-class gentlemen doing business on South Centre Street (South Main). Pomeroy, Dives, and Stewart's modern department store (red brick) was across the street at the southeastern corner of Mahantongo (Lantenengo) and Centre (Main) Streets. It could cater to the visitors' and residents' needs and wants.

This view looks up Norwegian (Christiana Street) from Railroad Street (Railroad Avenue) to Centre Street (Main).

O'Hara claimed: . . . Railroad Avenue was the street of dives; the intersection of Christiana Street and Railroad Avenue was the local capital of crime and violence. (*Ten North Frederick* 131)

At the beginning of the century, the vehicular traffic of horse-drawn buggies and carts was a usual sight on Centre (Main) and Market (Market) Streets. In the roadwork of the day, the trolley tracks can be seen rounding the corner up Market Street.

In Joseph B. Chapin's time, the trolley cars went west up Market Street. One could catch the trolleys at Garfield Square on Market Street or the railroad depot on East Norwegian Street near Chapin's home between 1890 and 1932. (*Pottsville Sesquicentennial 1806–1956*, 64)

The Young Men's Christian Association on Market and Second Streets had as one of its directors a gentleman of the calibre of William Dilworth English (B.S. Lafayette College; M.D., University of Pennsylvania) in the late 1920s. (*Appointment in Samarra* 51;53) When John O'Hara was a teenager, he would try to "pen" a letter "amidst the clamour and tumult of the famished crowd at the Y.M.C.A." (*Selected Letters of JOHN O'HARA*, John O'Hara to Robert Simonds, postmarked 3 March 1923, 5)

This south view from Arch Street shows Second Street with the Y.M.C.A. located on the west side of it. The Y.M.C.A's front is facing Market Street. Troy Laundry is situated in the same square on Second Street.

In the early 1900s, Carter Stokes Jr., a bachelor aristocrat, "lived at the Y.M.C.A. because it was cheap and respectable and offered the facilities of the swimming pool, the cafeteria, the barber shop, the New York and Philadelphia newspapers, and all of the standard American and English magazines."(*Ten North Frederick* 31)

This north view from Arch Street on North Second Street shows the Troy Laundry on the left, the clock tower of the Schuylkill County Courthouse, and the splendor of another day in 1912.

During the 1920s, the young author frequented The Pottville Free Public Library on the corner of Market and Third Streets to seek the advice of the renowned librarian, Edith Patterson. Before 1922, John O'Hara sought books in the cramped shelves of the library located at 208 West Market Street in a "one-time saloon." (*Pottsville Sesquicentennial* 1806–1956, 32)

In 1906, the First Methodist Church on Fourth and Market Streets was one of many denominations in Pottsville. Pottsvillians had a choice of religious affiliation from Catholic to Episcopalian doctrine in Schuylkill County's centre.

This view of Market Street at the turn of the century shows the eighth square with its houses and businesses lining the tree-lined street. This square was known for housing the Rettig C & Son Brewery between 816 and 822 Market Street. This location included its factory and office. O'Hara referred to the Rettig Brewery as the Rutters Brewery in *Ten North Frederick*. (W.H. Boyd, ed., *Boyd's Directory of Pottsville*, 1901–1903, 14; *Ten North Frederick* 282)

This parade in Garfield Square (two squares west of Second Street on Market) was typical of its day. Julian English's friends would spend time discussing a parade such as this. Garfield Square was formerly called Market Square. (*Pottsville Sesquicentennial* 1806–1956, 15) (*Appointment in Samarra* 149)

This view of Market Street from the west shows the tree-lined street with sidewalks and horse and buggy traffic in 1908. Note the stately tombstones in the Charles Baber Cemetery.

The burial service of Joseph B. Chapin of 10 North Frederick Street (North George) took place at the Charles Baber Cemetery on Market and Fourteenth Streets in 1945. The chapel and pond were on the cemetery's grounds when his forebears were buried in 1912. (*Ten North Frederick* 19-21)

Laurel Street with its sidewalks, shade trees, and framed houses was a delightful street to live on in 1908. This third square of Laurel Street was familiar to Pottsvillian Bernadette Koury Barket as a child. Her grandparents lived in the home adjacent to the telegraph pole.

Schuylkill County Prison (Lantenengo County Prison) was located at the back of the Courthouse at 230 Sanderson Street in Pottsville.

> . . . Lantenengo County Prison was ruled by a warden . . . And so when Al Grecco was sent up on the poorbox burglary matter he was not altogether unknown at the Stoney Lonesome, as the prison was called. (*Appointment in Samarra* 41)

The sober and dignified atmosphere of the Schuylkill County Courthouse, built in 1891, attracted lawyers such as Benjamin J. Chapin and Joseph B. Chapin of *Ten North Frederick* to present their cases within its walls. The courthouse and its clock could be seen from the back porch of John O'Hara's 606 Mahantongo Street home.

> . . . in twenty-six years she [Ruth Jenkins] had never been inside the courthouse. Every day of her life, practically, she looked at the courthouse clock and that ended it . . . (*Ten North Frederick* 85).

The armory located at the upper end of North Centre Street was utilized as an emergency hospital in the 1918 Influenza Epidemic.

... Mrs. Barlow, the leader of society, did not stop, and her husband knew better than to try to insist. She was charming and stylish and looked very English in her Red Cross canteen division uniform. She assumed charge of the emergency hospital in the armory and bossed the Catholic sisters and the graduate nurses around and made them like it ... (*The Doctor's Son And Other Stories* 32).

In O'Hara's youth, the staff of the police barracks (State Constabulary) reinforced law and order throughout Pottsville. Julian English and his gang of friends "would hop a wagon—preferably a packing-house wagon or a wholesale grocery wagon; coal wagons were too slow—and ride out to the state police barracks and watch the staties drill and shoot. . ." (*Appointment in Samarra* 149-150).

The site of the barracks was located on Ann Street, East Mines, St. Clair. Today, the building is still standing.

The Sheafer Building at 325 South Centre Street, Pottsville, housed the real estate, insurance, and general commission holdings of Frank J. Sheafer before the building was converted into a Y.W.C.A. (Samuel T. Wiley, *Biographical And Portrait Cyclopedia Of Schuylkill County Pennsylvania* 450) (*Pottsville Sesquicentennial 1806–1956*, 20)

Individuals such as wealthy Pottsvillians could deposit their monies at this regal-looking bank on Pottsville's South Centre and Union Streets' northwest corner. In the days of the Safe Deposit Bank Building, South Centre Street had cobblestone paving and shade trees. (*Pottsville Sesquicentennial 1806–1956*, 77)

The Penn Hall Hotel with its grand porches was a landmark on the corners of Howard Avenue and South Centre (South Main) Street. O'Hara's characters would stop in for the occasional drink when the opportunity arose.

The funeral services of Joseph B. Chapin in 1945 took place at Trinity Episcopal Church on South Centre (South Main) Street and Howard Avenue.

. . . The horns of protest during the twenty-minute [traffic] jam were not able to drown out the tolling bells of Trinity. Those noble bells had been tolling while those motor cars were still buried in the Mesabi Range, and they would continue to toll long after the last of those cars was junk. But the battle of the decibels made Gibbsville, at least for part of an hour, sound like a city . . . (*Ten North Frederick* 19).

In 1911, the Trinity Episcopal Choir sung hymns to the Stokes, the Chapins, and the Englishes of the upper classes of Gibbsville. (*Appointment in Samarra* 54)

> ... The Lockwoods of Swedish Haven [Schuylkill Haven] would naturally be Lutherans, and it was no more inconsistent for Lockwoods to be Lutherans than for the important German-name brewers and meat packers to belong to Trinity Church in Gibbsville. (*The Lockwood Concern* 135-136)

The Hotel Allan on Mahantongo (Lantenengo) and South Centre (South Main) Streets catered to the likes of Julian McHenry English everyday.

> He [Julian] finished his breakfast and drove downtown to the John Gibb Hotel [Hotel Allan; Necho Allen], where every morning he stopped to have his shoes shined ... (*Appointment in Samarra* 160).

Dives, Pomeroy & Stewart's Store would have, obviously, catered to an individual such as Lloyd Williams in *Ten North Frederick*.
 . . . All of his clothing was of good material and workmanship, all bought off the hanger at a Gibbsville men's store, none of it cheap or second-rate, and he achieved what he set out to do: through extreme care he gave the impression of a man who cared nothing about clothes; or for ceremony, or for side . . . (*Ten North Frederick* 77)

The Union Safety Deposit Bank at the corner of Mahantongo and South Centre Streets was one of many institutions that protected the upper class's money and taught its clientele how to be wise stewards of their money. (*Appointment in Samarra* 51)

The New Coal & Iron Company Building located at 200 Mahantongo Street in 1905 controlled the coal interests in "The Anthracite Region." "Anyone in Gibbsville who had any important money made it in coal; anthracite." (*Appointment in Samarra* 49)

The Pottsville post office was built in 1898 on South Second and Norwegian Streets in Dr. Patrick O'Hara's day. If this post office is noted for anything, it would be the "spotting" of John O'Hara's mother (Katharine Delaney) as a young girl in front of it by the young debonair Dr. Patrick H. O'Hara. This moment was priceless. O'Hara's father was noted for expressing that he would marry her one day. (Kathleen O'Hara Fuldner, John O'Hara Walking Tour, 17 September 1995) (Zerbey, *The History of Pottsville and Schuylkill County, Pennsylvania*, See Bibliography 337)

At the beginning of the century, the O'Hara family faithfully attended St. Patrick's Roman Catholic Church located next to the D.G. Yuengling Brewery on Mahantongo Street. In 1828, the first St. Patrick's Church was erected for $1,000 on O'Hara's Lantenengo Street. (*Pottsville Sesquicentennial 1806–1956, 67*)

The Pottsville Hospital was established in 1895. The following year Dr. Patrick O'Hara became its first resident surgeon. By 1915, Dr. Patrick H. O'Hara was surrounded by eminent physicians such as Dr. George H. Halberstadt, Dr. Joseph L. Warne, Dr. Oscar J. Carlin, Dr. J.B. Rogers, Dr. A.L. Gillars, Dr. G.H. Boyer, and Dr. J.J. Moore. (*Pottsville Sesquicentennial 1806–1956, 70*) (Farr, *O'Hara: A Biography* 27)

In John O'Hara's day, the Pottsville Hospital was known for serving the injured miners:

> . . . It was almost a day's drive from some of the mines to the hospital, in the mule-drawn-ambulance days. Sometimes the patient or patients would bleed to death on the way, in spite of the best care on the part of the first aid crews. Sometimes a simple fracture would be joggled into a gangrenous condition by the time the ambulance got off the terrible roads. But when that occurred Dr. English would amputate . . . (*Appointment in Samarra* 54).

There was no lack of hospital and nursing facilities in the early 1900s. A renowned doctor such as Dr. Patrick O'Hara served at its up-to-date hospital, and nurses used their modern skills to help the sick.

In 1888, the Tilt Silk Mill (named after the Tilt family) was the "first textile mill" to locate in Schuylkill County. By 1906, the Tilt Silk Mill on Laurel Street and Twelfth Street was considered one of the most important industries in Schuylkill County. In John O'Hara's heyday (1920s) in Pottsville, he danced with the Tilt Silk Mill girls at Maher's dance hall in Shenandoah. ("Reminiss?," *Pal Joey* 103) (Bassett, "O'Hara's Roots," *Pottsville Republican*, 9 October 1971; 14 August 1971)

This lucrative silk factory (Tilt Silk Mill) employed "as high as 1500 persons" in its heyday. One old-timer remarked: "It looked like a parade up Laurel and Market Streets" when the employees were released from work. Imagine this scene with 1,500 workers! (Anonymous interview, Pottsville gentleman, 107 North George Street, Pottsville, PA, 16 August 1996) (Zerbey, *The History of Pottsville and Schuylkill County, Pennsylvania*, See Bibliography 2121)

The Eastern Steel Mill located on Peacock Street between 1902 and 1931 was so imprinted upon O'Hara's mind that he mentioned it in *Ten North Frederick*. (*Ten North Frederick* 57) (*Pottsville Sesquicentennial* 1806–1956, 35)

Next to the power house is seen Sailor Pig Mill and Lumber Company located at 611–623 Mauch Chunk Street. O'Hara emphasized that some of Pottsville's wealth came from timber. (*Ten North Frederick* 57–58) (Zerbey, *The History of Pottsville and Schuylkill County, Pennsylvania* 2098–2099)

These shops located on Coal Street in Pottsville were owned by the Philadelphia & Reading Coal & Iron Company, which O'Hara spoke about in *Appointment in Samarra*. Irma Fliegler was pleased that her husband, Lute, sold automobiles at Julian English's Gibbsville-Cadillac Motor Car Company rather than work for the Coal & Iron Company. (*Appointment in Samarra* 4)

It was not an unusual sight to see a timber team such as this along the main arteries of Pottsville since timber was a source of excellent income for the upper-class families of Pottsville. (*Ten North Frederick* 57)

Three

The "Aristocrats'" Way of Life in Lantenengo County (Schuylkill County)

John O'Hara recorded:

> In Gibbsville, in 1909, only a few men could tell with exactness the true wealth of the wealthy Gibbsville families. A family that had assets worth $800,000 could, and usually did, live in great comfort without spending much more money than a family worth $200,000. It was a matter of pride with the best people of Gibbsville to live comfortably, but without the kind of display that would publicly reveal the extent of their wealth. A few families, whose names were given to large holdings in coal lands and to breweries and meat-packing houses, lived in American luxury. They were the owners of the early motor cars. They employed the larger staffs of servants. They had summer homes at distant resorts and led the lists of contributors to church and charity. Their wealth was a known fact and they were free to enjoy it. But behind them, obscured by the known wealthy, were the well-off, who possessed considerable fortunes and who quietly ran the town.
>
> The Benjamin Chapins were one such family. They lived within their income, they bought only the best and they bought to last . . . The Benjamin Chapins made no compromise with taste as they felt it or quality as they understood it. With those principles to guide them, they also privately believed, privately but firmly, that the very fact that an object was owned by them made it all right, good enough for anyone and too good for most. (*Ten North Frederick* 119-120)

In the lower left of the picture is the house (with the turret) of Charles Atkins, owner of The Pottsville Iron & Steel Company. This home is typical of the so-called "Aristocrats" of O'Hara's day who located themselves on the rather stately South Centre Street. (*Appointment in Samarra* 104)

The "Aristocrats," such as the Walkers in *Appointment in Samarra* or the Pottsvillian Charles Atkins, lived just beyond the shops (for example, Dives, Pomeroy, & Stewart) that Joseph B. Chapin of *Ten North Frederick* patronized on Centre Street. (*Appointment in Samarra* 104) (*Ten North Frederick* 306)

The mansions of Mahantongo Street (Lantenengo Street) inspired John O'Hara to write about Mahantongo Street in his first novel *Appointment in Samarra*. "Lantenengo Street had a sort of cottony silence to it." (*Appointment in Samarra* 2) By the 1920s, the New Wealth and the Children of the Old Wealth moved to the "Roads," "Places," "Drives," and Lantenengo Street on the "West Side of Gibbsville." (*Ten North Frederick* 105-106)

Residential Section—Mahantongo, West of 13th street, Pottsville, Pa.

Mansions such as this on Mahantongo Street (Lantenengo Street) belonged to the children of the old and monied families of North Frederick (North George) and South Main (South Centre) Streets. This view illustrates why the up and coming third-generation families desired to live on Mahantongo Street by 1909:

> In 1909 there were so many old, quite old houses on Lantenengo Street [Mahantongo Street] that Gibbsville did not need to have the still older residences of North Frederick Street [North George Street] and South Main [South Centre] . . . (*Ten North Frederick* 105-106).

On the upper reaches of Mahantongo square long estates were hidden behind rows of deciduous trees; for example, the Archbalds, Sheafers, and Yuenglings lived in such a lavish manner.

> . . . A few families, whose names were given to large holdings in coal lands and to breweries and meat-packing houses, lived in American luxury . . . (*Ten North Frederick* 119).

POTTSVILLE, PA.   6397 P

When ladies and gentlemen went shopping on Centre Street (Main Street) in the first half of the century, the ladies were properly attired in their dresses and hats, and the gentlemen in their suits, ties, white collars and hats. (*Ten North Frederick* 396; 112) During Edith Chapin's time, an upper-class woman dressed in a "skirt, blouse and ankle-length coat, following the natural waistline. The design was to make women look tall, with vertical stitching and piping to further the scheme. . . ." "Enormous, elaborate and expensive" hats enhanced the wearer's appearance. (*Ten North Frederick* 112)

J. Miehle & Son Department Store on West Norwegian and Centre Streets was the height of luxury in Edith Chapin's day. The main entrance to this delightful establishment is shown here. On 17 December 1914, this first-class department store burnt down. (Pottsville Sesquicentennial 1806–1956, 54)

J. Miehle & Son Department Store stretched back 230 feet from Centre Street to Second Street. Its Second Street entrance was a shortcut for the residents living on Mahantongo (Lantenengo) Street.

J. Miehle & Son Department Store was so modern for its day that it had a waiting room and passenger elevator for its clientele.

On the second floor of J. Miehle & Son Department Store, the shoppers of the day bought their fashionable cloaks to wear in Pottsville. (*Ten North Frederick* 20; 306; 112)

This section of J. Miehle & Son Department Store catered to the wants of the upper-class Edith Chapin: shirt waists, millinery, and infants' wear. (*Ten North Frederick* 112; 233-234)

This north aisle of J. Miehle & Son Department Store shows the men's "furnishings" of the day.

> . . . he [Joe Chapin] patronized Main Street [Centre Street] for socks and underwear, which gave him the opportunity to appear in the store, and gave the merchant the benefit of his patronage above the actual money spent . . . (*Ten North Frederick* 306).

This south aisle (230 feet deep) shows J. Miehle & Son Department Store's modern display cases with its expensive goods that its clientele enjoyed looking at and purchasing.

This shoe department of J. Miehle & Son Department Store could offer a proper fitting and tasteful shoe to its upper-class customers such as Edith Chapin from North Frederick Street (North George Street) and Waldo Wallace Walker from South Main Street (South Centre Street). (*Ten North Frederick* 246; *Appointment in Samarra* 195)

After his disgraceful conduct at the Stage Coach the night before, Julian English met Irma Fliegler on the narrow sidewalk outside Green's Jewelry Store (J.J. Gray's Jewelry Store) at 8 South Centre Street. (*Appointment in Samarra* 161-162) The jewelry at Green's was exquisite!

In 1908, all types of wagons were lined along the main business street (Centre Street) of Pottsville. When O'Hara was a youngster, the street was filled with them and the "gang" would take advantage of that fact. (*Appointment in Samarra* 149-150)

In 1908, a horseless carriage was parked near the entrance to the Charles Baber Cemetery on Market Street. Pottsville's wealthy families were able to buy such a luxury even though the country had just come out of the 1907 Depression.

This automobile with its side runners was a luxury back in the early 1900s in "The Anthracite Region." Note the attire of the gentleman leaning against the front of the motor car.

Only the wealthy had an automobile such as this in "The Anthracite Region" in 1914. John O'Hara recorded that the wealthy drove automobiles such as the Buick, Daniel, Dodge, Mercer Phaeton, Oakland coupe, Packard roadster, and Wills Ste. Claire in "The Region" by the 1920s and early 1930s. ("A Few Trips and Some Poetry" 42)

In 1914, this proud family would use this automobile on limited occasions to visit family on a Sunday or to tour "The Region" on Sunday drives.

Notice the trolley car in the middle of Centre Street (Main Street), Pottsville (Gibbsville), on a lovely day in 1907.

The upper-class Pottsvillians were driving the Dodge Brothers' automobiles from Detroit up and down North George and Mahantongo Streets in 1929–1930. O'Hara accurately described a Dodge's "loose cross-chain banging against the fender":

> Irma lay there, fully awake, and heard a sound: cack, thock, cack, thock, cack, thock . . . Then [the Dodge] came a little faster and the sound changed to cack, cack, cack, cack-cack-cack-cack . . . it was an open car . . . (*Appointment in Samarra* 3-4).

One can see the unpaved Gordon Nagle Trail which the early motorists of the century attempted to drive and the youthful John O'Hara rode on his horse, "Julia." When the young John O'Hara wanted to escape from Pottsville, he would ride "Julia" out to the "Farmers Hotel" and, then, continue on to his Father's farm in the Panther Valley. In later years, he would tour the area in an automobile with his friend and, at times, travel to Beckville (The Farmers Hotel) for a drink with the "Mockie" crowd. ("A Few Trips and Some Poetry" 37-38; 41-42; 90-91)

Four

The "Aristocrats'" Schooling Inside and Outside "The Region"

When O'Hara analyzed "The Region," he believed that the wealthy attended colleges such as Lafayette, Lehigh for engineering, Muhlenberg, the University of Pennsylvania, and Yale. Most colleges in the East or Middle West were represented in Gibbsville, but Harvard College seemed to be the exception. (*Ten North Frederick* 58) O'Hara came to the conclusion that in Gibbsville, the "University" meant the University of Pennsylvania in Philadelphia. But most families felt Philadelphia was too far away from Gibbsville. They wanted their sons to go to nearby colleges in smaller towns such as Allentown (Muhlenberg), Carlisle (Dickinson), and Easton (Lafayette). The feeling was that Yale was a New England institution and Princeton was too strongly Southern. Families whose sons had a pre-Pennsylvania New England background sent their children to Yale, for instance, Joseph B. Chapin. (*Ten North Frederick* 149)

If O'Hara referred to the individual's preparatory school days, he placed his Gibbsville's upper-class sons in schools from Mercersburg to The Hill in Pottstown; his upper-class daughters in schools from Spence in New York to St. Timothy's in Stevenson, Maryland; however, O'Hara revealed "The Region's" overwhelming influence on these well-schooled "Aristocrats":

> "Well, all those years before we went away to school, we were learning all about the people and the geography, the streets, the names of the towns and patches. You might say we took a course in Gibbsville. Why throw that out the window? No, I'd never work in New York, not permanently. I'll go to work in Father's firm, . . ." (*Ten North Frederick* 151).

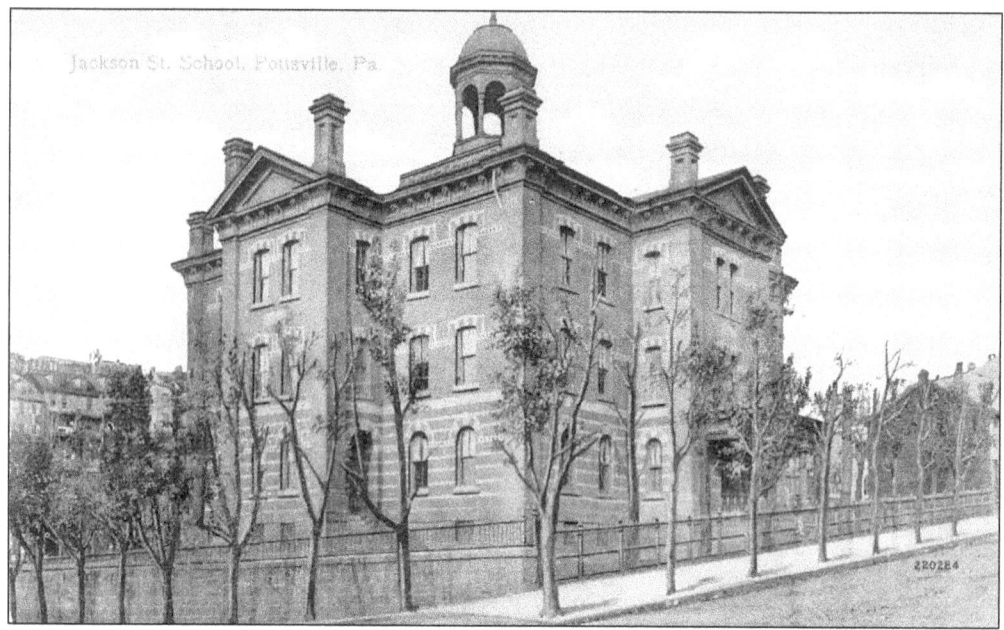

The lower- and middle-class children of Pottsville attended the Jackson Street School located at 500 East Norwegian Street and North Jackson Street on Pottsville's East Side in O'Hara's day. Joby Chapin from North Frederick Street (North George Street) would encounter these children when playing out in front of the Nonpareil Hose Company Number 2 (Phoenix Hook & Ladder Company, 320 East Norwegian Street) (*Ten North Frederick* 241-242)

Bunker Hill School, located in the seventh square of Schuylkill Avenue, catered to the lower- and middle-class children of Pottsville in O'Hara's day. In 1853, it had the distinction of being Pottsville's first high school with 30 students in one room. It would be very likely that only the parents with money could have their children attend in the 1850s. (*Pottsville Sesquicentennial 1806–1956*, 36)

In 1913, Garfield High School (Pottsville's High School) on Pottsville's West Side was rather impressive. Its teachers catered in comfortable surroundings to the educational needs of the children. It was customary for the upper-class Gibbsvillians of O'Hara's day to attend private day schools; however, they competed with Gibbsville High school in "baseball" and in a "dual track meet" when the occasion arose. (*Ten North Frederick* 282-283)

In 1933, Pottsville High School was built on Sixteenth Street and Elk Avenue. Joseph B. Chapin's law partner, Arthur McHenry, wanted his son to go to Gibbsville High School. ". . . If I had a son, which I never will, I'd send him to Gibbsville High and Penn State." (*Ten North Frederick* 199)

In Joseph Chapin's youth, the youngsters of St. Clair attended this high school in St. Clair and competed against "Gibbsville High." (*Ten North Frederick* 282-283)

The Hill School Chapel was an institution where young gentlemen (Joseph B. Chapin and Arthur McHenry) prayed for God's blessing and guidance.

O'Hara's wealthier friends on the upper reaches of Mahantongo Street went to The Hill School established in 1851 in Pottstown, Pennsylvania—the very kind of school that he wished that he could have attended. Rich individuals such as Alfred Eaton in *From the Terrace* and Joseph B. Chapin in *Ten North Frederick* were part of the alumni of The Hill School.

O'Hara's character, Robert Millhouser from Lyons (Lykens), went to Mercersburg Academy in Mercersburg when he was a young lad. (*Ourselves to Know* 10)

When Robert Millhouser of *Ourselves to Know* attended prep school, he, probably, sauntered along this Walk near South Cottage at Mercersburg Academy during his school days. (*Ourselves to Know* 10)

Surely, Dr. Patrick O'Hara took his son to his alma mater, The University of Pennsylvania, and its dormitories when they visited Philadelphia. According to John O'Hara, when an individual spoke of "The University" in Pottsville, he, of course, was thinking of The University of Pennsylvania. (*Ten North Frederick* 149)

The University of Pennsylvania was founded in 1740 by Benjamin Franklin as a charitable school. In 1875, the "University" was re-located west of the Schuylkill River in Philadelphia.

These dormitories of the University of Pennsylvania were the home to many of the young Pottsvillian students at the turn of the twentieth century. They were opened in 1896 and at that time could accommodate 630 students.

Possibly, the grandeur of the entrance to the dormitories of O'Hara's father's university (University of Pennsylvania) spurred O'Hara on to bring to light the "halls of learning" in Pennsylvania throughout his Pennsylvania novels.

This is another striking view of the dormitories of the University of Pennsylvania in Philadelphia at the turn of the century.

Joseph B. Chapin and Arthur McHenry would have passed by Byers Hall and even frequented it in their school days at Yale. Yale was so much on the mind of John O'Hara that Joseph B. Chapin announced that his son, Joby Chapin, would be "the fifth in line to go to Yale, fifth generation, and maybe more . . ." (*Ten North Frederick* 198-199).

John O'Hara would have loved to attend Woodbridge Hall at Yale University in his youth. Because of his love for Yale, O'Hara became engrossed with the pomp and circumstance of America's universities.

A school such as Lafayette College in Easton, Pennsylvania, educated Pottsvillians or Gibbsvillians such as William Dilworth English and his son, Julian McHenry English, in *Appointment in Samarra*. Julian English would have seen this hall, Pardee Hall (named after a coal baron from "The Anthracite Region") when he strolled about the campus.

Dr. William Dilworth English (B.S.) and Julian McHenry English would have seen football games at a stadium similar to this during their school years at Lafayette College in Easton, Pennsylvania. (*Appointment in Samarra* 51; 53) In 1927, O'Hara and his gang attended various college football games at this large stadium known as "Fisher Stadium." In O'Hara's day, Lafayette College and grounds were situated on top of the hill known as "College Hill." (*Selected Letters of JOHN O'HARA*, John O'Hara to Robert Simonds, August 1927, 20) (Staff of Skillman Library. Lafayette College, telephone interview, Pottsville, Pennsylvania to Easton, Pennsylvania, 21 September 1999)

Excited Pottsvillian students congregated at this station during term breaks, for instance Christmas, to await the arrival of a train to take them home to "The Region" where various holiday festivities would take place.

When Julian English and his Lafayette College crowd got together during the week and on the weekends, North Fourth Street in Easton would be filled with the jovial group. Without a doubt, John O'Hara, Fred Hoefel, and the "Purity Gang" would have gathered here if they went to a football game at Lafayette. (*Selected Letters of JOHN O'HARA*, John O'Hara to Robert Simonds, August 1927, 20)

The wealthy of Pottsville went to Lehigh University in Bethlehem, Pennsylvania, to earn a degree in engineering. These boys would, unquestionably, have attended the Packer Memorial Chapel during their stay at Lehigh. Even though Bethlehem was known as a "steel town," Lehigh's students enjoyed an ivory-tower existence. (*Ten North Frederick* 58)

Dr. Schwenk, the pastor of the Lutheran church, and Judge Flickinger in *Ten North Frederick* would have attended classes in the Administration Building when they went to Muhlenberg College in Allentown, Pennsylvania, in the early part of the century. (*Ten North Frederick* 199)

This is another view of the Administration Building at Muhlenberg College, Allentown, Pennsylvania. In 1905, this building's architecture was considered quite attractive for its day.

The Berkes (Berks) Hall Building, Muhlenberg College, Allentown, Pennsylvania, was built in 1903 to house the students on their return on 3 January 1904. It was considered "sheer luxury" with its "open fireplace" and its "hot showers" at the turn of the century. Today, it is part of East Hall, Muhlenberg College. (Michael Bruchner, Vice-President of Public Relations, Muhlenberg College, telephone interview, Pottsville, Pennsylvania to Allentown, Pennsylvania, 19 August 1999)

Families such as the McHenrys would have marvelled at an earlier scene of the courthouse on the public square when they took their son, Arthur, to attend Dickinson's "first-rate law school." If Arthur had a son, he, surely, would have appreciated this image of the courthouse that his father once laid eyes on. (*Ten North Frederick* 149)

Dickinson College enrolled an individual such as Arthur McHenry from Gibbsville to study at its renowned Law School and then return to South Centre (South Main) Street to practice as an attorney. (*Ten North Frederick* 149)

John O'Hara attended Keystone State Normal School in Kutztown, Pennsylvania, in the schoolyear of 1921–1922. He was dismissed. In O'Hara's way of thinking, this Normal School was a far cry from his beloved Yale. (*Selected Letters of JOHN O'HARA*, Chronology, xv)

This brick building housed the principal during his term at Keystone Normal School in Kutztown, Pennsylvania, in the 1920s.

One of the sights for Sidney Tate of Fort Penn (Harrisburg) to behold during the time that Paul Reichelderfer invited him to Lebanon, Pennsylvania, would be the boys' dormitory at Lebanon Valley College, Annville, Pennsylvania.

Swarthmore College would have been a likely college for the upper-class children of "The Region" to enter. Parrish Hall with its tranquil appearance led one to believe that the institution had a conducive environment for learning.

In 1907, Raymond Hall, Vassar College, attracted the daughters of the wealthy. Perhaps, a Pottsvillian escaped from the "Coal Region" to this remarkable haven in Poughkeepsie, New York.

Lady Janes School in Binghamton, New York, would be similar to the types of finishing schools that O'Hara's female characters would attend to obtain the polish that they required to associate with the upper classes in Pottsville in Edith Chapin's day.

In all likelihood, O'Hara's mother, Katharine Delaney, had a school trip to Poquessing Creek when she was enrolled at Eden Hall, Convent of the Sacred Heart, in Torresdale, Pennsylvania. (Bruccoli, *The O'Hara Concern* 8)

Five

THE "ARISTOCRATS'" SOCIAL ENCLAVES AND ESCAPES

John O'Hara was so aware of Pottsville's aristocracy that he knew that this close-knit milieu needed their very own clubs and escapes to survive in an area surrounded by "those hideous coal mines. Those mountains of coal dust and those shabby little villages, and the gouges in the land . . ." (*The Lockwood Concern* 353). O'Hara, passionately, related the particulars of the Schuylkill Country Club (Lantenengo Country Club), the Pottsville Club (Gibbsville Club), and The Second Thursdays, an exclusive dinner-party arrangement once a month: November, December, January, February, and March at the homes of the "really substantial people." (*Ten North Frederick* 230-233)

Throughout his Pennsylvania novels, novellas, and short stories, O'Hara provided details about the "Aristocracy's" escapes. Whether it was Tumbling Run, two miles from Pottsville or Eagles Mere, Sullivan County, O'Hara knew the wealthy's fashionable resorts and parks where they would gather. The younger set of the "Aristocrats" would zoom off to various dance halls, hotels, parks, pavilions, roadhouses, and theatres, inside and outside "The Region" in their own automobiles and their families' automobiles: Wills Ste. Claires, Packard roadsters, Oakland coupes, Mercer phaetons, Daniels, Dodges, and Buicks. ("A Few Trips and Some Poetry" 42) From Lakewood Park to Asbury Park in New Jersey, the "Aristocrats" took full advantage of the marvellous opportunities awaiting them: bathing, dancing, rowing, walking or just relaxing. The "Aristocrats'" enclaves and escapes offered nothing but the best for the families that contributed to "The Region" and O'Hara made it his business to know about the "best."

The Pottsville Club (Gibbsville Club) was re-located to 314 Mahantongo Street, Pottsville, on November 16, 1910. Being a member of the Gibbsville Club (Pottsville Club) did not give ready access to the Lantenengo Country Club (Schuylkill Country Club) or the tennis club (Out Door Club). (Zerbey, "Pottville Club Moved to New Home," 17 November 1933: 120-122) (*Ten North Frederick* 229-230) If a Christian man "made his money in a sanctioned enterprise and did not habitually leave his car parked in front of whorehouses, [he] could be reasonably sure of election to the Gibbsville Club within two years of proposal and seconding . . ." (*Ten North Frederick* 230).

This elite private club (Out Door Club; O'Hara's tennis club), located on Oak Road and its tennis courts situated on Howard Avenue, entertained the likes of Dr. and Mrs. O'Hara before the founding of the private Schuylkill Country Club (Lantenengo Country Club) in 1920. (*Ten North Frederick* 229-230)

"Gibbsville, in the first two decades of the Twentieth Century, suffered from a sense of shame because of its lack of a country club. The existence of the tennis club [Out Door Club], which was, from the standpoint of exclusiveness, far superior to any of the country clubs in comparable Pennsylvania towns, did not make up for the fact that until 1920, Gibbsville gentlemen had to motor to the next county if they wished to play golf . . . Anyone who belonged to the tennis club had made the club grade in Gibbsville. . ." (*Ten North Frederick* 229-230).

It was seven miles and just a little over from the country club [Schuylkill Country Club in 1930] to the Gibbsville Bank & Trust Building [Mahantongo & South Centre Streets] and practically all of the last three miles was a new and nearly straight stretch of road, which had been easier to clear; it was protected from winds by a railroad embankment on one side... (*Appointment in Samarra* 19).

The Elks' Home, located in the third square of Mahantongo Street (Lantenengo Street), catered to the middle classes of Pottsville. W. Carl Johnson remarked:

... But now the Gibbsville Club has a waiting list [1945] as long as your arm and some fellows would like to have a place to go that isn't the Elks... (*Ten North Frederick* 58).

The elegant lobby of the Necho Allen Hotel (John Gibb Hotel) with its terrazzo floors, marble columns, and moreen-finished walls catered to the upper class of Pottsville in the late 1920s and early 1930s. (*Appointment in Samarra* 33)

Fairway No.1 at Irem's Playground (Irem Temple), Dallas, Pennsylvania, was an escape to the coal barons (if they so desired) that lived in the Scranton and Wilkes-Barre area. It reminded one of the Schuylkill Country Club's (Lantenengo Country Club) golf course:

> . . . In the summer the golf course was so neatly shaved that it made him think of a farmer in his Sunday suit surrounded by other farmers in overalls and straw hats . . . (*Appointment in Samarra* 72).

The attractive entrance to Tumbling Run Park lured the "Aristocrats" of Pottsville to come out to enjoy Tumbling Run's hotel, dance pavilion, auditorium, and sandy beach in 1910.

Tumbling Run, two miles from Pottsville, was a once-famous amusement park for all classes of people in Pottsville; however, its boathouses would house the young "Aristocrats" of "The Region," for instance Joseph B. Chapin of Gibbsville (Pottsville) and J.B. Westervelt, Martha Sterling Downs's cousin. (*Ten North Frederick* 137) (*The Lockwood Concern* 150)

These boathouses at Tumbling Run were owned by the "Aristocrats" of the day.

> "They (Westervelts) have one of the nicest boathouses at The Run. One of the few that you can live in. You know what The Run is? It's a reservoir, an artificial lake, owned by the coal company, and people like J.B. Westervelt get the very best boathouses . . . (*The Lockwood Concern* 150). The shores were lined with boathouses, elaborate and simple. The Chapin boathouse was not one of the simple places . . . (*Ten North Frederick* 137).

The beauty of the park and lake at Tumbling Run attracted the "Aristocrats" (for instance, The Chapins of Gibbsville and The Lockwoods of Swedish Haven (Schuylkill Haven) to enjoy the park's hotel, or its rowing, or its bathing in the cool, refreshing waters of the "artificial" lake. Note the fashionable attire of the ladies and gentlemen in 1909. (*Ten North Frederick* 137) (*The Lockwood Concern* 150)

Tumbling Run Lake with its sandy beach was known for its cold water which the visitors found quite refreshing.
"... You'll enjoy it, if you don't mind bathing in cold water." (*The Lockwood Concern* 150)

This scene of Tumbling Run shows how lovely the lake could be on a summer day. At times, the park had its serene moments.

This view of Tumbling Run from the north side captures the tranquillity of the moment. Tumbling Run was peaceful for a brief interlude for Abraham Lockwood and Martha Sterling Downs.
. . . Now they [Abraham Lockwood and Martha Sterling Downs] could hear voices . . . The music puffing out of the carrousel in the casino at the eastern end of the dam. The bell on the large launch that was about to make its hourly tour of the dam. The air whistle on the electric railway car from Gibbsville echoing down the valley. (*The Lockwood Concern* 155)

. . . He [Abraham Lockwood] took her [Martha Sterling Downs] for a spin in the naphtha launch, tied up the launch on the south shore of the dam [Tumbling Run] where there were no boathouses but in full view of the boathouses on the north shore . . . (*The Lockwood Concern* 155).

Carousel, Tumbling Run, Pottsville, Pa.

The carousel at Tumbling Run was located at the east end of the dam. Lovers on the south shore of the dam could hear its music when they were off on their own in the woods. (*The Lockwood Concern* 155)

Even though the Tumbling Run Hotel at Tumbling Run was known for its festive moments, one could find peace and quiet at this quaint and unpretentious haunt. This scene illustrates its tranquillity.

O'Hara's characters such as Abraham Lockwood and Martha Sterling Downs would have surely walked down this path (Lovers' Lane, Tumbling Run) when engaging in a love affair. (*The Lockwood Concern* 157)

Lovers such as Abraham Lockwood and Martha Sterling Downs would gaze upon The Run's water from the bridge at the head of Tumbling Run. (*The Lockwood Concern* 157)

Marlin Park was another escape for the wealthy of "The Region." This park, located in the town of Marlin, Pennsylvania, had the Marlin Dam to soothe the hot visitors of the day. Perhaps, the wealthy Isabel Barley and her lover, Jim, went to this romantic spot near Minersville (Collieryville). ("A Few Trips and Some Poetry" 105)

The opulent Lakeside Hotel at Eagles Mere, Pennsylvania catered to the wants of the upper-class Pottsvillians in 1910. Individuals in the Chapin family would, likely, dine and rest here during the long, hot summer months.

In Eagles Mere, the "Aristocrats" of Gibbsville always attended a church on Sunday when they resided at the Lakeside Hotel or one of the summer cottages. The wealthy Pottsvillians (Gibbsvillians) of the day probably visited this Presbyterian church in 1915.

In 1910, the Baptist Church of Eagles Mere had its share of tourists and residents. Children could not wait to go to Sunday school every week at this quaint church.

In 1911, this tranquil scene of the lake at Eagles Mere could give a feeling of peace to an aristocratic family such as the Chapins.

One could row, swim, or sight-see at Eagles Mere during Joe Chapin's later years in the 1940s.

This view from the pier illustrates the attraction of Eagles Mere with its sandy bathing beach and impressive bathhouse. The "Aristocrats" of Pottsville, for instance Joseph B. Chapin, went to Eagles Mere, Sullivan County, Pennsylvania, to swim and relax during the long, hot summer days in "The Region."

In 1921, this picturesque lane guided the "Aristocrats" to Eagles Mere's golf links where one could play a round of golf to lessen the tension of everyday life.

In 1916, these cottages with their tree-lined street in Eagles Mere Park would house the "Aristocrats" of "The Region" during the stifling summer months. To the right of the scene, note the gentleman in his white flannels and jacket. The women on the left are dressed in cool summer attire.

Schuylkill Park was located just outside of the town of Port Carbon on Highway 209. It was a spot for Pottsvillians (Gibbsvillians) to walk or automobile or trolley out to in 1921. Its various amusement rides, for instance the giant roller coaster and Ferris wheel, attracted the residents of Pottsville (Gibbsville). ("Reminiss?," *Pal Joey* 103) (*Pottsville Sesquicentennial 1806–1956*, 76)

Pottsvillians (Gibbsvillians) swam in the modern swimming pool at Schuylkill Park. While swimming, they would be able to hear the sounds of music floating through the air and the noises of the amusements nearby. ("Reminiss?," *Pal Joey* 103) (*Pottsville Sesquicentennial 1806–1956*, 76)

Pottsvillians (Gibbsvillians) could just dream while watching the ducks on the lake at Schuylkill Park. No longer can the people of Pottsville (Gibbsville) fantasize at this park; it has gradually faded away like its counterpart, Tumbling Run. ("Reminiss?," *Pal Joey* 103) (*Pottsville Sesquicentennial 1806–1956*, 76)

In this scene, one can see the dancing pavilion in the background. Its ballroom with its dance bands would entice people to come from all over "The Region." If one did not want to dance, one could canoe in its refreshing lake and still hear the sounds of music while rowing. ("Reminiss?," *Pal Joey* 103) (*Pottsville Sesquicentennial* 1806–1956, 76)

When John O'Hara wanted to dance and have fun, he, often, went with his boyhood friends to Lakewood Park near the popular spots of Hazleton, Tamaqua, Mahanoy City, and Shenandoah, Pennsylvania, to mix with "The Region's" young women and to see such exciting personalities as Mr. Paul Whiteman perform. (*Selected Letters of JOHN O'HARA*, John O'Hara to Robert Simonds, August 1927, 19)

This bird's-eye view of Lakewood Park located between Mahanoy City and Tamaqua illustrates the beauty of such an escape during John O'Hara's day. One could enjoy the rather quiet activity of rowing at Lakewood Park besides partaking in its dancing and exciting band entertainment.

When John O'Hara wanted to escape from Pottsville, he went to such parks as this one. Even his character, Pal Joey, entertained at this scenic park called Manila Park (Manila Grove) located in the wooded section below the hospital on Kline's Hill in the area called "Seek" in Coaldale. Its dance pavilion with its swinging music attracted the young and old in the 1920s and 1930s. ("Reminiss?," *Pal Joey* 103) (*Selected Letters of JOHN O'HARA*, John O'Hara to Robert Simonds, October 1932, 70) (Staff of Tamaqua Free Public Library, telephone interview, Pottsville, Pennsylvania to Tamaqua, Pennsylvania, 19 August 1999)

This extraordinary view of Mauch Chunk from Flagstaff could relieve the anxiety of any "Coal Region" resident. Located just a few miles from Pottsville, it could be an "escape" for the "Aristocrats" of Pottsville (Gibbsville) in John O'Hara's day.

This pavilion located at Memorial Park, East Mauch Chunk, entertained the youth of "The Region." The beauty that surrounded the pavilion would have delighted the young and the old.

In 1910, a family would go on a picnic at Coney Island near Ashland. Rowing would be a common sight around the island. The romantic scenery of Coney Island drew many couples to row in their leisure. Maybe, the O'Hara family had the occasion to take in its beauty.

If Pottsvillians (Gibbsvillians) went to Shamokin, they could row on Edgewood Lake. Even as a young child, O'Hara liked to leave Pottsville to learn something new. Presumably, he had the opportunity of going to this lake.

Pal Joey and his so-called colleagues would hold their musical sessions at Island Park in Harrisburg (Fort Penn). O'Hara and his gang loved to go to Island Park to hear the music of the day. In this scene in 1910, the spectators are concentrating on watching the track. Likely, betting is involved in the racing activity! ("Reminiss?," *Pal Joey* 103)

Lafayette was O'Hara's William Dilworth English's and his son Julian's alma mater. It is with certainty that one could say that Julian and his father would have visited Island Park situated on an island south of Easton. Island Park was opened on 19 July 1894, became an amusement park in 1904, and closed in 1919 due to the trolley trestle being destroyed by an ice floe. (*Appointment in Samarra* 51; 106) (Sharon Gothard, staff, Marx Room, Easton Area Public Library, telephone interview, Pottsville, Pennsylvania to Easton, Pennsylvania, 20 August 1999)

Julian English and his gang from Lafayette College would have been entertained at this pavilion in Bushkill Park, Easton, when wanting to leave the school or even the coal dust of "The Region." On 1 July 1902, Bushkill Park opened near Bushkill Creek. In Julian's day, the dance hall would have been the top priority on the gang's list. By 1928, Bushkill's dance hall of Julian's school days was destroyed. Today, Bushkill Park is still in operation. (Sharon Gothard, staff, Marx Room, Easton Area Public Library, telephone interview, Pottsville, Pennsylvania to Easton, Pennsylvania, 20 August 1999)

The middle and upper classes of Pottsville went on excursions to Atlantic City, New Jersey, during the summer months. In this scene, the young children were pretending to row their boat in the sand.

> Ruth Jenkins had lived all her life in Gibbsville, never had been out of the Commonwealth of Pennsylvania except for two one-day excursions to Atlantic City, . . . (*Ten North Frederick* 85).

Pottsvillians (Gibbsvillians) went to bathe at Atlantic City, New Jersey, during the hot and humid summer of 1909. Note the crowded beach. (*Ten North Frederick* 85)

Robert Millhouser of Lyons (Lykens) and other wealthy families vacationed at Asbury Park, New Jersey. They bathed in the water or walked the Boardwalk or just sat out on the sand to enjoy the sun and the salty, cool air of the Atlantic Ocean. Note the attire of the ladies and gentlemen in the earlier part of the American Twentieth Century. (*Ourselves to Know* 322)

This picturesque scene of the reservoir at Lykens (Lyons) would attract the lovers of 1908. Undoubtedly, Robert Millhouser and Hedda saw this setting during their courting days. (*Ourselves to Know* 234)

Likely, John O'Hara would be familiar with this west branch of the reservoir at Lykens when he went to see his grandparents (Delaneys) at 635 North Main Street, Lykens. (Kathleen O'Hara Fuldner, telephone interview, Pottsville, Pennsylvania to Lenoir, North Carolina, 21 February 1994)

Maybe this romantic scene in Lykens inspired Robert Millhouser to fall in love with Hedda in his middle age. (*Ourselves to Know* 236;258-259)

As a young man, O'Hara could not wait to listen to the "city noises" in Philadelphia in the early hours of the morning. (*Selected Letters of JOHN O'HARA*, John O'Hara to Robert Simonds, October 1932, 69)

When O'Hara went with his parents to Philadelphia, he loved to stay at the Bellevue-Stratford Hotel. (*Selected Letters of JOHN O'HARA*, John O'Hara to Robert Simonds, October 1932, 69) A character such as Mrs. Carter Stokes of the STOKES family of Gibbsville "stayed at the Bellevue-Stratford" in the early part of the twentieth century. (*Ten North Frederick* 188)

When O'Hara was a young boy, his father would take him on an outing to Philadelphia to shop at Wanamaker's, one of Philadelphia's department stores that catered to the wealthy.

Edith Chapin loved to shop at Wanamaker's: "I have a great deal of shopping to do tomorrow. There's a sale at Wanamaker's and this will be my last chance to get a lot of things done for the fall . . ." (*Ten North Frederick* 245)

The Philadelphia and Reading Pennsylvania Railroad Station was the terminus in Philly where the Chapins and Williams of *Ten North Frederick* would deboard to be taxied off to the Bellevue-Stratford for a long needed rest. (*Ten North Frederick* 245-247)

No doubt, Sidney Tate saw the Cornwall and Lebanon Railroad Depot in Lebanon, Pennsylvania, when he went to Lebanon to look at nearby farms and to celebrate the Christmas holidays. (*A Rage to Live* 74; 77; 81)

When Sidney Tate of *A Rage to Live* visited Paul Reichelderfer, he would have seen this majestic-looking church (St. Luke's Episcopal Church) in Lebanon, Pennsylvania.

The Clarks Ferry Bridge connected the Susquehanna Trail and Wm. Penn Highway. It was located in the village of Clarks Ferry (Becksville). O'Hara graphically denoted the composition of Clarks Ferry in the early 1900s during Grace Caldwell Tate's day in A Rage to Live:
. . . "an occasional stone quarry, a farmers' hotel, a church (Episcopal), a flour-mill, a general store, a blacksmith shop, and a couple of dozen homes . . . ."
If a visitor from "The Region" was invited to the Tates, they sometimes went to the farm located in this vicinity adjacent to "The Region." Today, it is difficult to realize that this quaint village of Clarks Ferry even existed. (A Rage to Live, 9; 142-143) (Wilson R. Dumble, review of A Rage to Live, by John O'Hara, "The Engineer Bookshelf," The Ohio State Engineer 1949: 17, 38)

The Pennsylvania Railroad Station in Harrisburg (Fort Penn) was a spot that the likes of the upper class, for instance Sidney Tate in A Rage to Live and Robert Millhouser or Ben Rosebery in Ourselves to Know, utilized in their business and social life. (A Rage to Live 77) (Ourselves to Know 29; 214)

Pottsvillians (Gibbsvillians) would go to Reading to frequent the places such as the Raja Temple or a theatre such as the Orpheum. Bands and dancing would entertain the young adults at these halls during O'Hara's era. (*Selected Letters of JOHN O'HARA*, John O'Hara to Robert Simonds, postmarked 12 December 1927, 26-27)

In 1908, Spruce Street in Shamokin was a rather pleasant, quiet street to walk along in the daytime. Perchance, O'Hara with his "Purity League" gang visited this town in one of his adventurous moments in the 1920s! To leave boring Pottsville was O'Hara's goal in those days.

When O'Hara visited his friends, Catherine and Robert Simonds in Allentown, Pennsylvania, he could not miss the sight of the Lehigh Canal.

This Mt. Gretna scene shows the young boys at drill during the Great War. During World War I, individuals such as Arthur McHenry and Joseph B. Chapin discussed the possibility of joining the National Guard. It would be, at least, a release from the coal patches surrounding Gibbsville (Pottsville); however, Arthur McHenry's sentiment was this:

"I'd rather wait awhile and see what happens. I don't want to have to drill, and go to camp at Mount Gretna, and march in parades everytime a Civil War veteran dies," . . . "Drudgery," said Arthur. (*Ten North Frederick* 198)

This is another view of the land surrounding the Schuylkill County Almshouse and Hospital for Insane near Schuylkill Haven. Note the Almshouse Farm located to the left of the scene. The Hospital for Insane may have been an "escape" from the well-knit and tightly knit conventions of the "Aristocrats'" world. Only, the Lockwood girls would know! (*The Lockwood Concern* 106)

The Third Brigade Band served as an escape for the "Aristocrats" and "The Region's" inhabitants. It was a delightful experience to see the band marching down Pottsville's (Gibbsville's) Centre Street (Main Street). No doubt, the young John O'Hara would have been very caught up with the patriotic songs that this band would play; even his character, Julian English, loved a good parade. (*Appointment in Samarra* 149) (Bruccoli, *The O'Hara Concern* 19)

When the middle- and upper-class Pottsvillians (Gibbsvillians) escaped to Fifth Avenue, New York, to shop, it was considered a "gladsome encounter" to see another Gibbsvillian; however, the Pennsylvania Dutch mayor of Gibbsville (Conrad L. Yates) believed "his block on South Main Street [South Centre Street, Pottsville] was a New Yorker's on Fifth Avenue . . ."(*Ten North Frederick* 97; 246).

When Caroline was trying to convince her husband, Julian English, to conduct himself properly at the Lantenengo Country Club (Schuylkill Country Club), she mentioned that she would "[go] out in the car with [him] at intermission and stay with [him], the way [they] used to." It would be similar to the time that the Englishes stayed at their escape, Lake Placid, New York, which is seen in the image. (*Appointment in Samarra* 71)

John O'Hara's first trip to Europe was as a steward on the S.S. *George Washington* in June and July 1927; however, the "Aristocrats" of Pottsville (Gibbsville), for instance Joseph B. Chapin and family, planned their first-class voyages abroad a year ahead of time. This escape was the height of luxury for the "Aristocrats" of Pottsville, Schuylkill County (Gibbsville, Lantenengo County), Pennsylvania, and "The Anthracite Region" in the early 1900s. (*Selected Letters of JOHN O'HARA*, Chronology, xv) (*Ten North Frederick* 290-291)

Bibliography

O'Hara, John. *Appointment in Samarra*. 1934. New York : First Vintage, 1982.
O'Hara, John. *The Doctor's Son And Other Stories*. New York: Harcourt, 1935.
O'Hara, John. "Reminiss?." *Pal Joey. The Novel and The Libretto and Lyrics*. 1940. New York: First Vintage, 1983.
O'Hara, John. *A Rage to Live*. 1949. New York : Carroll & Graf, 1986.
O'Hara, John. *Ten North Frederick*. 1955. New York: Carroll & Graf, 1985.
O'Hara, John. *From the Terrace*. Introduction by Budd Schulberg. 1958. New York: Carroll & Graf, 1993.
O'Hara, John. *Ourselves to Know*. 1960. New York: Bantam Books, 1967.
O'Hara, John. "Imagine Kissing Pete." *Sermons and Soda-Water*. 1960. New York : Carroll & Graf, 1986. 3-12.
O'Hara, John. Foreword. *Sermons and Soda-Water*. By O'Hara. 1960. New York: Carroll & Graf, 1986. N. pag.
O'Hara, John. *The Lockwood Concern*. 1965. New York: Carroll & Graf, 1986.
O'Hara, John. "A Few Trips and Some Poetry." *And Other Stories*. 1968. New York: Bantam, 1970.
O'Hara, John. *Lovey Childs*. London: New English Library, 1972.
O'Hara, John. *Selected Letters of JOHN O'HARA*. Ed. Matthew J. Bruccoli. New York: Random, 1978.
O'Hara, John. "The Doctor's Son." *Gibbsville, PA*. Preface by George V. Higgins. Introduction by ed. Matthew J. Bruccoli. New York: Carroll & Graf, 1992.

UNPROCESSED LETTER
O'Hara, John. Letter to Miss Mary Connelly. 16 June 1962. John O'Hara Papers. The Rare Books Room. Pattee Library. Pennsylvania State University. State College, Pennsylvania.

PROCESSED POSTCARD
O'Hara, John. Postcard to Robert Simonds. July 1927. John O'Hara Papers. The Rare Books Room. Pattee Library. Pennsylvania State University. State College, Pennsylvania.

NEWSPAPERS
Advertising recorded in the *Tamaqua Evening Courier* 1 February–21 March 1927.
Bassett, Charles W. "O'Hara's Roots." *Pottsville Republican* 20 March 1971–8 January 1972.
Collector's Edition. "The Pottsville Hospital and Warne Clinic." "Hospital founded in 1895 to serve community needs." *Pottsville(PA.) Republican & Evening Herald* Saturday-Sunday, 4–5 November 1995: 3-4.
Zerbey, Joseph Henry, *The History of Pottsville and Schuylkill County, Pennsylvania*. Republished from Pottsville 'Evening republican' and Pottsville 'morning paper' (J.H. Zerby newspapers, inc.) during the fiftieth anniversary year of these publications, from October 22, 1933, to October 21, 1934, and concluded in 1935 . . . Pottsville, 'Republican'-'Morning paper' print, 1934–1935. "Pottsville Club Moved to New Home." 17 November 1933, 120-122.

DISSERTATIONS
Coakley, Thomas Patrick. " 'O'Hara Country' Revisited: A Study of Regionalism, Theme and Point of View In The Work of John O'Hara." Ph.D. Dissertation. Pennsylvania State University, 1983.
Mac Arthur, Pamela C. "John Henry O'Hara's View Of The Upper Classes In Pennsylvania Between

1900 and 1930." M.A. Dissertation. University of Alberta, 1986.

Mac Arthur, Pamela C. "John O'Hara: A Biographical Study." D.Phil. Dissertation. University of Sussex, Brighton, England, 1999.

INTERVIEWS

Anonymous Interview. Pottsville gentleman. 107 North George Street, Pottsville, Pennsylvania, 16 August 1996.

Barket, Bernadette Koury. Telephone interview, Schuylkill Haven, Pennsylvania to Pottsville, Pennsylvania, 8 May 1999. Various interviews took place between the months of May and July 1999 about "The Anthracite Region."

Bruchner, Michael, Vice President of Public Relations, Muhlenberg College. Telephone interview, Pottsville, Pennsylvania to Allentown, Pennsylvania, 19 August 1999.

Drumheller, Elmer. Telephone interview, Pottsville, Pennsylvania to Port Carbon, Pennsylvania, 19 July 1999.

Gothard, Sharon. Staff, Marx Room, Easton Area Public Library. Telephone interview, Pottsville, Pennsylvania to Easton, Pennsylvania, 20 August 1999.

O'Hara Fuldner, Kathleen. Telephone interview, Pottsville, Pennsylvania, to Lenoir, North Carolina, 21 February 1994

Sharadin, Jane. Telephone interview, Pottsville, Pennsylvania, 19 July 1999.

Staff of Skillman Library. Lafayette College. Telephone interview, Pottsville, Pennsylvania to Easton, Pennsylvania, 21 September 1999.

Staff of Tamaqua Free Public Library. Telephone interview, Pottsville, Pennsylvania, to Tamaqua, Pennsylvania, 19 August 1999.

REVIEW

Dumble, Wilson R. Review of *A Rage to Live*, by John O'Hara. "The Engineer Bookshelf." *The Ohio State Engineer* 1949: 17, 38

TOUR

O'Hara Fuldner, Kathleen. John O'Hara Conference. John O'Hara Walking Tour. Mahantongo Street, Pottsville, Pennsylvania, 17 September 1995.

BOOKLETS

Pottsville Sesquicentennial 1806–1956. Pottsville, PA: The Historical Society Of Schuylkill County, 1956.

Hanney, Joseph M. *Pottsville Bicentennial 1776–1976*. Pottsville: Pottsville Bicentennial Association, 1976.

BOOKS

Boyd's Directory of Pottsville Including Yorkville, Palo Alto, Mt. Carbon and Mechanicsville. Ed. W.H. Boyd. Reading, Pa.: W.H. Boyd, 1901–1903.

Bruccoli, Matthew J. *The O'Hara Concern: A Biography of John O'Hara*. 1975. Pittsburgh: University of Pittsburgh Press, 1995.

Davies II, Edward J. *The Anthracite Aristocracy: Leadership and Social Change in the Hard Coal Regions of Northeastern Pennsylvania, 1800–1930*. DeKalb, Illinois: Northern Illinois Press, 1985.

Farr, Finis. *O'Hara: A Biography*. Boston: Little, 1973.

Strange, Charles. *Mountain Majesties: An Historical Novel 1927–1937*. Pottsville: J.F. Seiders Printers, 1996.

Swain, James E. *History of Muhlenberg College*. New York: Appleton-Century-Crofts, 1967.

Wiley, Samuel T. *Biographical and Portrait Cyclopedia of Schuylkill County, Pennsylvania*. Ed. Henry W. Ruoff. 1893. Rev. ed. Mt Vernon, In.: Windmill Publications, 1993.

Visit us at
arcadiapublishing.com

www.ingramcontent.com/pod-product-compliance
Lightning Source LLC
Chambersburg PA
CBHW080859100426
42812CB00007B/2085